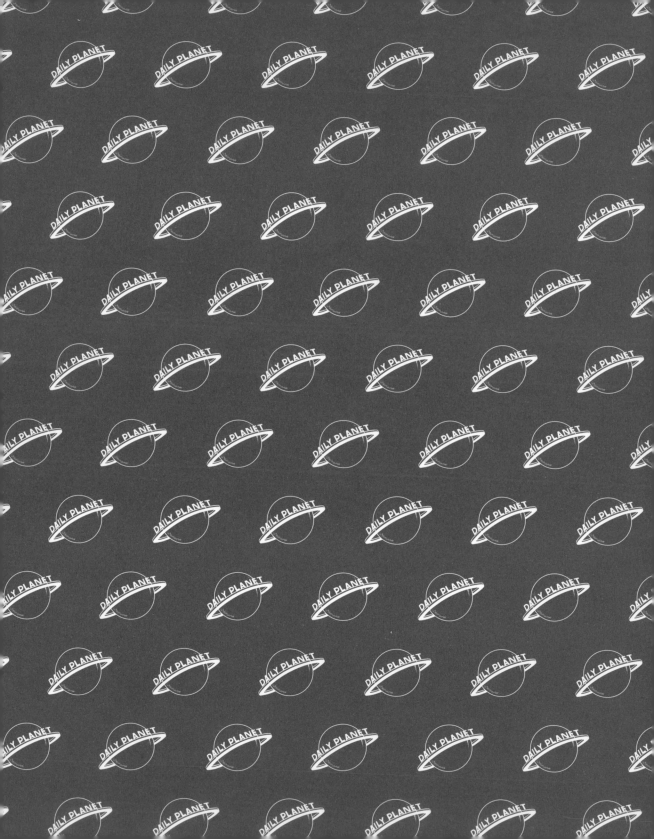

DAILY PLANET

By Matthew K. Manning

a division of
INSIGHT EDITIONS
San Rafael, California

INTRODUCTION

THERE EXISTS PERHAPS NO BETTER introduction to the world's first true superhero than this classic intro from the *Adventures of Superman* television show from the 1950s. Evolved from a similar voiceover that launched Superman's 1940s radio show, the introduction captures the main bullet points of the revered Man of Steel. While his life as Superman and his alien background are fascinating, perhaps the most defining attribute of the Last Son of Krypton's personality is his secret alter ego as a mild-mannered reporter. Unlike many other modern-day super-heroes, Superman is judged by his integrity both in and out of his bright, classic tights. And to know Clark Kent is to also know his place of employment, the other bastion of truth and justice in the troubled city of Metropolis: the *Daily Planet*.

Immortalized in comic books, television shows, video games, and films, the *Daily Planet* building stands as a permanent fixture in the Metropolis skyline. The *Daily Planet* is Clark Kent's home away from home. As the base of operations for the city's most trusted newspaper, the building is a bustling center for many heroes in the field of journalism, people who serve to continually inspire Superman's ongoing war against evil. The *Daily Planet* is a major part of Superman's life, with a history as rich and involved as the Man of Steel's own.

THE COMPANY THAT WOULD become known as DC Comics first debuted as National Allied Publications. Its first official comic book was *New Fun*, a black and white collection of all-new comic strips, cover-dated February 1935. This was an innovation for the time, as before *New Fun*, the only comic books to be found on the stands were collections of previously published newspaper strips. Comic strips were an extremely popular form of entertainment in newspapers, so when *New Fun* offered material readers had never before seen, the idea caught on in the fledgling comic book market. However, National Allied Publications still didn't have a hit on its hands. The company had no breakout character to call its own.

Inspired by the extremely popular newspaper adventure strips of the day, writer Jerry Siegel and artist Joe Shuster collaborated on a new comic idea, one with a science fiction spin. Their creation was Superman, and when they sold the concept as a comic book instead of a newspaper strip, the emerging comics industry would be forever changed. Not only was Superman born, but so was the concept of the superhero.

Superman debuted in *Action Comics* #1 (June 1938) and was an instant success. Featured on the magazine's cover lifting a car above his head, this unique character, wearing a bright red cape and blue tights, was unlike anything readers had ever seen. On page one of his first thirteen-page

THE DAILY STAR OFFICE IS REACHED...

YOU WANTED TO SEE ME?

YES, BE SEATED

REPORTS HAVE BEEN STREAMING IN THAT A FELLOW WITH GIGANTIC STRENGTH NAMED SUPERMAN ACTUALLY EXISTS. I'M MAKING IT YOUR STEADY ASSIGNMENT TO COVER THESE REPORTS. THINK YOU CAN HANDLE IT, KENT?

LISTEN, CHIEF, IF I CAN'T FIND OUT ANYTHING ABOUT THIS SUPERMAN NO ONE CAN!

story, Superman's origin was quickly told for his hungry audience. The lone survivor of a distant planet, Superman was rocketed to Earth as an infant and adopted his role as a "champion of the oppressed" when he realized he was much mightier than the inhabitants of his new world. Still a work in progress, Superman could not fly in his original appearances. He could, however, leap an eighth of a mile, raise "tremendous weights," and outrun an express train. These powers were explained by the fact that the denizens of his home planet simply had physical structures millions of years more advanced than those of the people of Earth. This superpower origin was later explained by declaring Krypton a planet that revolved around a red sun. When Superman traveled from this planet to Earth, the radiation from Earth's yellow sun was what imbued the hero with his strange and wonderful abilities.

From his very first appearance, Superman was already a reporter in his alter ego of Clark Kent. His boss, later to be named George Taylor, was the editor-in-chief of the *Daily Star*, a newspaper that would serve as the blueprint for

the *Daily Planet* in years to come. *Action Comics* #1 also debuted Lois Lane, the Man of Steel's famous love interest and Clark Kent's rival reporter at the *Daily Star*. While Clark seemed smitten with her from her very first panel, Lois only had eyes for Superman. Thus began one of comics' most memorable and enduring love triangles.

BEARING LOIS IN HIS ARMS SUPERMAN HEADS TOWARD THE CITY ——

By June of 1939, only one year after his debut in the anthology title *Action Comics*, Superman was rewarded for his popularity with a second comic book title. Entitled simply *Superman*, the comic featured multiple Superman stories compared to the one lone tale featured in *Action Comics*.

Superman was originally released on a quarterly schedule, but the title would soon advance to a bimonthly schedule, and later, a monthly one. (The current *Superman* series is released twice a month.) In the pages of that classic *Superman* #1 issue, readers were treated to the story of just how Clark Kent secured his job at the *Daily Star*. After being turned down for a position by the *Star*'s editor-in-chief, Clark Kent learned the scoop behind a near lynching and called the *Daily Star* to report it. Having proved his newspaperman chops, Clark was quickly offered a reporter job at the *Star*. While the inside of the paper's offices was shown in *Action Comics* #1, the *Daily Star*'s exterior wasn't revealed until *Action Comics* #12 (May 1939). Even then, the building was only shown at street level, its cornerstone looming in the background behind Clark Kent.

Superman would receive a third title when *World's Finest Comics* (originally *World's Best Comics*) debuted in 1941. This title included not just new Superman material, but also adventures of DC Comics' other hit, Batman, a character whose very creation was inspired by Superman's popularity.

But Superman's success was not just limited to the pages of comic books. His first true mainstream exposure was earned in real-life newspapers when the *Superman* daily comic strip debuted on January 16, 1939. In this Golden Age of comic books, newspaper strips were considered the "big leagues," read by tens of millions of adults and children every day, much more than the average comic book that was geared at the time to appeal only to kids. It was this newspaper strip that would give the *Daily Star*'s editor-in-chief George Taylor his name, and it was this newspaper strip that decided to change the name of the *Daily Star* to the *Daily Planet*.

By *Action Comics* #23 (April 1940), the comic books followed suit, and the *Daily Star* began to fade into obscurity.

But Superman's popularity didn't end there. He soon earned his own hit radio show in 1940 and a series of cartoons in 1941. Both would contribute significantly toward the Superman mythos as well as the budding legend of the *Daily Planet*. The radio show changed the name of the *Daily Planet*'s editor-in-chief from George Taylor to Perry White. Meanwhile, the Superman cartoon showcased the first exterior shot of the *Daily Planet* building. An art-deco masterpiece topped with a globe, the *Daily Planet* building became nearly as visually memorable as the red-and-blue-clad hero himself. The building soon found its way into comic books, its exterior debuting in the pages of *Superman* #19 (November–December 1942), and it has remained a mainstay in the skyline of Superman's town of Metropolis ever since.

Just as the *Daily Planet* was evolving into the institution known by Superman fans today, so too was Superman. He soon gained the ability to fly, he became so powerful that an atomic bomb couldn't kill him, and his senses became more enhanced, including super-hearing, scent, and x-ray vision. He developed super-breath and super-ventriloquism and even had adventures as a youth in the pages of *More Fun Comics* #101 (January–February 1945) as the similarly costumed Superboy. These adventures of Clark Kent set in the past later earned their own self-titled series in 1949. In the second issue of *Superboy*, it was revealed that the farm town Clark Kent had been raised in as a child was named Smallville.

Superman was comic books' undisputed star in the Golden Age. Several members of his Rogues Gallery sprouted up in this era, including his arch foe Lex Luthor, who began not as a bald billionaire, but rather as a red-haired inciter of wars. Also of note was the mad scientist known as the Ultra-Humanite, the mystical imp from the 5th dimension named Mr. Mxyzptlk (spelled Mxyztplk in his first appearance), and the Toyman, a villain who used classic toys to battle Superman and perform bizarre robberies.

In 1952, the *Adventures of Superman* TV program debuted, cementing the hero's reputation as the world's greatest hero in the eyes of the public. But near the end of that show's run in 1958, comic books were undergoing a transition. The Golden Age was giving way to what would become known as the Silver Age. And while several of DC Comics' characters were getting a makeover, the Man of Steel wasn't about to deviate from his brave course.

CLARK KENT

While all the details weren't known in his first appearance in *Action Comics* #1, Clark Kent's origin has been told and retold dozens of times over the decades. As a mere baby, Kal-El was sent to Earth by his parents, Jor-El and Lara. Arriving in a rocket from his native planet, Krypton, he landed in Smallville, Kansas, to be raised by the kindly Jonathan and Martha Kent. Years later, he made his way to the big city of Metropolis and found work at the *Daily Planet*, the city's greatest newspaper. With fantastic powers and few weaknesses aside from Kryptonite—radioactive rocks from Krypton's core—he fights for justice on two fronts, as mild-mannered reporter Clark Kent and as Superman, the Man of Steel!

LOIS LANE

Superman was a revolutionary character and comic books' first proper superhero. But Lois Lane was just as revolutionary. From her start in *Action Comics* #1 (June 1938), she was an independent, career-driven reporter. A feminist with strong opinions and an even stronger moral core, Lois went on to star in her own series in the 1950s entitled *Superman's Girl Friend, Lois Lane*. The series would last nearly two decades at a time when female-led comics were a rarity. Still a permanent fixture in Superman's life today, Lois even married the Man of Steel, the two later having their own super-son named Jonathan.

PERRY WHITE

While Superman's original editor at the *Daily Planet* was George Taylor, that particular editor-in-chief didn't keep his job for long. In *Superman* #7 (November–December 1940), Clark Kent and Lois Lane received an assignment from a redheaded chief called "Mr. White." This was the first appearance of Perry White in comics, although he had been previously mentioned on the Superman radio show. Over the years, Perry's history and family were expanded upon, a history that even included a rivalry with Superman villain Lex Luthor. A former reporter himself and a man of great integrity, Perry White continues today as a staunch advocate of Superman.

JIMMY OLSEN

The Daily Planet's cub reporter made his debut in *Action Comics* #6 (November 1938) as "an inquisitive office-boy," although he wasn't named in that issue. In fact, like many parts of Superman's world, Jimmy was truly established on the Superman radio show. In 1954, he gained his own long-running title, *Superman's Pal, Jimmy Olsen*, which ran until 1974, when the comic book's title was changed to *The Superman Family*. Jimmy has evolved into a world-class photographer, often getting himself into the kind of trouble that requires the help of Superman.

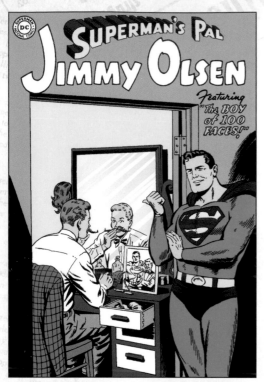

BY THE LATE 1950s AND EARLY 1960s, Superman had cemented his place in pop culture. And just as when he debuted, Superman's heroic life was complemented by Clark Kent's noble pursuit of truth and justice as a newspaperman. The *Daily Planet* was as firmly a part of Superman's life as it had been originally—in fact, arguably more so, as his supporting cast (most employed by the paper) became stars in their own right. Lois Lane and Jimmy Olsen gained their own ongoing Superman titles in the pages of *Superman's Girl Friend, Lois Lane* and *Superman's Pal, Jimmy Olsen.*

With more titles to tell the Last Son of Krypton's past and present adventures, several "untold tales" made their way into print. In the pages of *Superman's Pal, Jimmy Olsen* #36 (April 1959), readers learned just how Jimmy got his job at the *Daily Planet*. As it turns out, he was offered the job by Superman when the Man of Steel learned that, due to a bizarre time-traveling incident, Jimmy Olsen had been his babysitter briefly on Krypton.

Not to be outdone, Clark Kent's own employment origin was once again depicted in *Superman* #133 (November 1959). When his origin story was first told in the pages of *Superman* #1, Clark had originally been hired for nabbing a story about an attempted lynching, but in this retelling, Clark was hired by editor-in-chief Perry White after memorizing every *Daily Planet* scoop in the last thirty years. Impressed by Clark's knowledge, Lois Lane even argued on his behalf, and Kent was rewarded with an assignment at the local zoo. While Perry believed the zoo story to be a wild goose chase for Kent, Clark proved him wrong by dressing as a gorilla and performing super stunts.

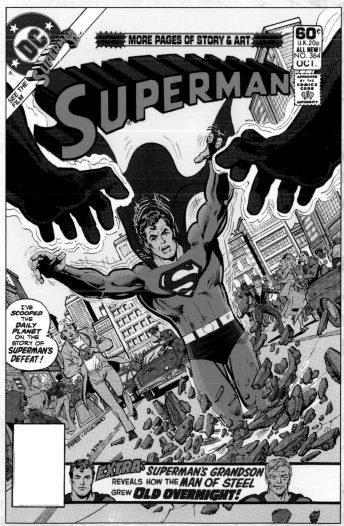

These types of light-hearted and far-fetched stories were typical of the Silver Age. Nevertheless, many of Superman's main foes debuted during this era, including the backwards Superman equivalent dubbed Bizarro, the alien mastermind Brainiac, the power-sapping Parasite, the metal monstrosity Metallo, and the renegade Kryptonian General Zod. Superman's visual style underwent a makeover as well. He evolved from the realistically proportioned figures of Joe Shuster's illustrations to the more impressive boxy-chest look personified in the work of artists Wayne Boring and Curt Swan. Superman's adventures extended into the fun-filled exploits of his "Superman Family" as well, from his Kryptonian cousin, Supergirl, to an array of super-pets, including Krypto the Superdog and Streaky the Supercat.

In the midst of all the fun and games, few people predicted the drastic changes ahead for the Man of Steel and his coworkers at the *Daily Planet.* Because as the 1970s arrived, Clark Kent would do the unthinkable: He would leave his job as a newspaper reporter.

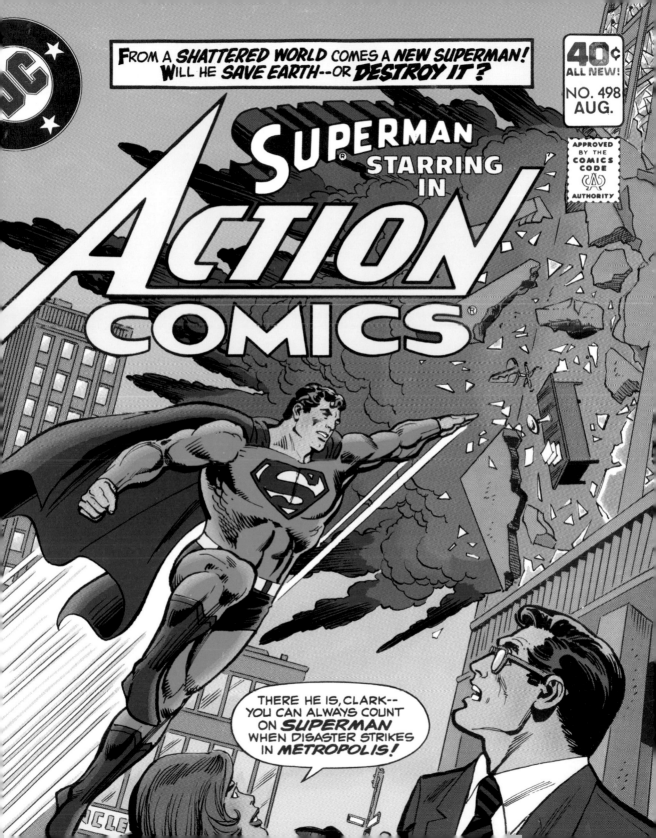

THE COMIC BOOK READERSHIP was changing, and the face of comic books was changing right along with it. In the 1960s, college kids embraced comics like never before. By the 1970s, adults were even enjoying the same titles they grew up reading as kids. This new readership demanded an examination of the medium, and soon, a more realistic approach to cartooning came into vogue in the comic book world. Nowhere was this more apparent than on artist Neal Adams's legendary cover for *Superman* #233 (January 1971).

Known now as a key issue in this emerging Bronze Age of comics, *Superman* #233 championed itself as "A Return to Greatness!," rocking the status quo of Clark Kent's normally stable work life. In this issue, Clark Kent was given a new type of reporting job as a TV reporter for the *Daily Planet*'s new owner, Morgan Edge.

Reporting for WGBS, Clark was soon removed from his job at the *Daily Planet* altogether, despite protests from Perry White. Edge wanted Kent for his TV station, and there was little Kent could do unless he wanted to lose his job altogether. Under the masthead of Galaxy Communications, Clark became a successful news anchor, joined in *Superman* #317 (November 1977) by his childhood friend Lana Lang at the anchor desk.

While Clark Kent's new job certainly altered his world, other worlds were also evolving during this era. DC Comics had begun to embrace the idea of multiple Earths, other planets existing in parallel dimensions with strange differences from the main comic book universe readers were familiar with. In *Justice League of America* #73 (August 1969), the Superman of Earth-2 was first referred to as such.

Every adventure in which Superman partook during the Golden Age of comics was retroactively regulated to this so-called Earth-2. This allowed the Superman of the 1970s (living on Earth-1) to still retain his youth and vitality. Earth-2's Superman was the Man of Steel active during the 1940s, and he later even married Lois Lane. This explained the seeming contradictions in continuity. Earth-1's Superman worked at the *Daily Planet*. Earth-2's Superman worked at the *Daily Star*. Earth-2's Superman would even get a raise in *The Superman Family* #196 (July–August 1979), when he was promoted to editor-in-chief (taking over for George Taylor).

New threats began to rear their ugly heads in Metropolis and beyond. Not the least of which was Darkseid, a demigod from the planet Apokolips who commanded an entire army of new and bizarre supervillains. The Atomic Skull challenged Superman to several blazing-hot battles, and the world-conquering Mongul made his way into Superman's new team-up title, *DC Comics Presents*.

In 1978, Superman once again flew into the public's eye, this time with the first in a series of four blockbuster live action films. Meanwhile, comic book writers continued to delve into the untold secrets of Superman's past. In *The New Adventures of Superboy* #12 (December 1980), Superboy met Perry White for the first time when the young reporter learned of the Boy of Steel's flight patterns and flagged him down.

The two became allies, and Superboy even told White his origin, giving Perry perhaps the greatest scoop in newspaper history. In the miniseries *Superman: The Secret Years* #4 (May 1985), the Perry White/Superboy relationship was examined once more when White investigated Superboy's disappearance. After alerting the Boy of Steel to Lex Luthor's latest evil plan, White was promoted to editor-in-chief of the *Daily Planet*.

In that same issue, Clark Kent made his way to Metropolis, interviewed for a job as a reporter at the *Daily Planet*, and was hired by White after Perry learned that, like Superboy, Clark Kent hailed from Smallville.

But as *The Secret Years* came to a close, a crisis had struck the DC Universe, signaling an end to the Bronze Age. *Crisis on Infinite Earths* was a massive twelve-issue crossover at DC that caused a huge shake-up to continuity. Earth-2 and Earth-1 were merged into a single Earth, and the Golden Age Superman escaped death to seemingly live happily ever after with his world's Lois Lane. Superman's world was about to be reshaped, and as the Man of Steel's history was to be retooled for a new generation, so too was the history of the *Daily Planet*.

IN THE MID-1980s, COMIC BOOKS WERE receiving a level of critical acclaim unheard of in the medium's history. Sophisticated works of writing and artistry were being created for a new generation of readers, and DC Comics was leading the pack. Writer and artist John Byrne was tasked with redefining Superman and his history for this new era, and he began his take with *The Man of Steel* six-issue miniseries, debuting in 1986. This served as a perfect jumping-on point for fans, and jump on they did.

In *The Man of Steel*, Superman's entire continuity was restarted from scratch. As the hero's strength levels were reduced slightly, and extraneous characters like Supergirl and the Super-Pets were relegated to comic book limbo, Superman's arch foe, Lex Luthor, was reinvented as a corrupt millionaire businessman, rather than the mad scientist of the Bronze Age who was often seen wearing a trademark green battle suit. What's more, it was Clark Kent who first nabbed the exclusive story on Superman's origin, a story that got him his job at the *Daily Planet*.

The *Daily Planet* continued to be a major part of Clark Kent's life throughout the modern era. In 1988, the fictional newspaper received its first in-continuity edition, a magazine-sized special that tied into DC's major *Invasion* miniseries. This faux newspaper came complete with articles written about the *Invasion* tie-in titles, fake ads, and even a comic strip section.

Lois Lane, Jimmy Olsen, and Perry White had been once again established as major supporting characters for Superman. Lois Lane learned Superman's identity and became engaged to the Man of Steel.

Perry White's backstory was fleshed out more than ever, and his family life was examined. Jimmy Olsen received nationwide acclaim for his powerful photograph when he captured the dramatic moment of Superman's untimely death. During a battle with the alien creature Doomsday, Superman was killed while defending the streets of Metropolis. Olsen snapped the picture of Superman's death, boosting sales for the *Daily Planet* despite its staff mourning their terrible loss.

Luckily for Metropolis, Superman would fight his way back from the dead, and the Man of Steel would return with renewed vigor. In fact, Clark Kent soon married Lois Lane in a ceremony in *Superman: The Wedding Album* #1 (December 1996) that was attended by nearly the entire *Daily Planet* staff.

Superman was kept plenty busy in this Modern Age, fighting the threats of new villains like the magical Silver Banshee and the android Cyborg Superman. All the while, his adventures were reported in the *Daily Planet*. The newspaper itself even became the subject of several major storylines as Superman's saga crossed over through each of his various titles. During "The Fall of Metropolis" event in the super-titles beginning in 1994, Lex Luthor was dying and opted to take Metropolis with him. To that end, he fired a series of sophisticated torpedoes at the city, causing the *Daily Planet* building's iconic globe to topple to the street below. But this didn't stop the dedicated newspaper team from continuing their work, even if they had to temporarily relocate to the *Daily Planet*'s printing press in the Queensland borough of Metropolis.

...d when this city bleeds, ...eeds red, yellow and blue.

Whatever Happened to the City of Tomorrow?

Hit with hard financial times, in the *Superman: Save the Planet* special (October 1998), the *Daily Planet* was sold to Lex Luthor, who then shut the paper down to absorb its employees into his online news source, LexCom. Lois Lane was able to talk Luthor into selling the paper back to Perry White in exchange for killing a future story of his choosing. Soon after, another financial player entered the game when Bruce Wayne—known to readers as Gotham City's Batman—bought the *Daily Planet*.

The newspaper's iconic building received a facelift during the Y2K event in Metropolis, when an upgraded Brainiac 13 reformed the city into a literal city of the future. Nowhere was this change more apparent than to the *Daily Planet* building's exterior. The iconic planet positioned atop its roof became a 3D holographic image for a time, matching the building's new streamlined appearance.

Nearly twenty years had passed since Superman's last update in the pages of *Man of Steel*. To keep the Last Son of Krypton fresh in the minds of readers, the *Superman: Birthright* miniseries was released, a twelve-issue series by writer Mark Waid and artist Leinil Yu that updated Clark Kent's origins as a reporter. In that series, the *Daily Planet* earned a new publisher in the form of the gruff Quentin Galloway.

However, in just a few short years, Superman's origins were once again rewritten in another miniseries, *Superman: Secret Origin*. This six-issue series by writer Geoff Johns and artist Gary Frank combined many elements of Superman's past and even ideas introduced in the original *Superman* film from 1978. With heavy focus on the *Daily Planet* and its staff, *Secret Origin* also retold the origin of the famed Metropolitan newspaper. In this updated version, the *Daily Planet* had fallen on hard times, and it wasn't until Lois Lane interviewed the Man of Steel, giving him the name Superman in the process, that the paper began to soar in the sales department. In this new origin, not only did the *Daily Planet* help make Superman a household name, but Superman's fame helped the *Daily Planet* reach iconic status as well.

THE NEW HIRES

As the Modern Age of comics slowly crafted a more realistic newsroom at the *Daily Planet*, many new employees emerged.

PERRY WHITE – EDITOR IN CHIEF. PERRY WHITE HAS WORKED AT THE DAILY PLANET SINCE HE WAS JIMMY OLSEN'S AGE. HE LIVES AND BREATHES NEWS. ALTHOUGH HE PRESENTS A GRUFF EXTERIOR AND OFTEN LECTURES HIS STAFF ON HOW IT WORKED IN "HIS DAY," PERRY CARES ABOUT EACH AND EVERY ONE OF THEM LIKE FAMILY. HE SEES LOIS AS HIS DAUGHTER IN MANY WAYS. HE CAN'T FOR THE LIFE OF HIM FIGURE OUT WHY CLARK DOESN'T TAP INTO THE GREATNESS PERRY SEES IN HIM MORE OFTEN.

STEVE LOMBAR... FOOTBALL IN HIG... LOMBARD SEES ... ISN'T, IN FACT. ... AND PUT-DOWNS ... HERSELF AT HIM...

CAT GRANT – GOSSIP AND FASHION COLUMNIST. IF THE MAYOR'S SLEEPING WITH SOMEONE BEHIND HIS WIFE'S BACK, CAT GRANT KNOWS ABOUT IT. CAT PRIDES HERSELF ON KNOWING EVERYONE'S PERSONAL BUSINESS IN METROPOLIS. BRILLIANT, SHE OFTEN USES HER LOOKS TO GET INTO MOST PLACES MOST PEOPLE DON'T WANT HER. SHE STILL CAN'T FIGURE OUT WHAT SUPERMAN EVER SAW IN LOIS OR WHY CLARK KENT NEVER LOOKS BELOW HER NECK.

RO... RO... EL... "TO... AC... HE... BL...

CLARK KENT – REPORTER. OFTEN MISTAKENLY THOUGHT FOR ABSENT-MINDED OR AWKWARD, CLARK IS ACTUALLY USING HIS SUPER-SENSES TO MONITOR METROPOLIS. ALTHOUGH HIS FELLOW STAFFERS GREATLY RESPECT HIS WORK (WELL, EXCEPT FOR LOMBARD, BUT HE DOESN'T RESPECT ANYONE'S WORK) CLARK HAS FEW PEOPLE HE CAN CALL FRIENDS AT THE DAILY PLANET. BECAUSE SUPERMAN'S POWERS OCCA-SIONALLY INTERFERE WITH COMPUTERS, CLARK IS FORCED TO WORK ON A TYPEWRITER.

LOIS LANE – REPORTER. LOIS LANE IS KNOWN AS THE ONLY REPORTER SUPERMAN GIVES INTERVIEWS TO. ONCE A LOW-LEVEL REPORTER CRAMPED IN A DESK IN THE CORNER BEHIND THE COFFEE MACHINE, LOIS LANE MADE HER NAME WITH HER REPORTS AND EDITORIALS CONDONING SUPERMAN AND CONDEMNING LEX LUTHOR.

JIMMY OLSEN – PHOTOGRAPH... PHOTOGRAPHER SUPERMAN WIL... JIMMY HAS THE LENS CAP ON. ... CLARK. JIMMY HAS THE GREATN... THE DAILY PLANET WILL EVER HA... CONSTANTLY PLAGUE JIMMY AN... ADVENTURES, UNDERAPPRECIATE... DAILY PLANET STAFF. JIMMY HA... SUPERMAN'S GREATEST ASSETS...

R. STEVE LOMBARD PLAYED
AND BRIEFLY FOR THE PROS.
MAN, EVERYTHING CLARK KENT
CLOPEDIA OF SPORTS TRIVIA
RE OUT WHY LOIS DOESN'T THROW

AL EDITORIALIST.
T HIGHLY EDUCATED REPORTER
MORE AWARDS THAN ANYONE
FACT, MANY PEOPLE SEE HIM AS
Y PLANET. RON IS AN AVID
UPS TO LIST. RON OFTEN BUTTS
ARD ON NOT NEARLY EVERYTHING,

KNOWN AS THE ONLY
NATELY HALF THE TIME
ST LIKE PERRY SEES
E THE BEST REPORTER
E AND SELF-DOUBT
IM, DESPITE HIS
Y MOST OF THE
TINUE TO BE ONE OF
S JOB.

CAT GRANT

FRANKLIN STERN

Cat Grant became established as the paper's gossip reporter, and Franklin Stern became the newspaper's publisher. Ron Troupe served as a lead political columnist, and Steve Lombard, a former anchor from the Galaxy Communications days of the 1970s, began his story anew as a sportswriter. Other additions to the *Daily Planet*'s staff included marketing consultant Simone D'Neige, all-around office busybody Allie Kesel, and even the vigilante Creeper in the guise of his alter ego, outspoken reporter Jack Ryder.

STEVE LOMBARD

CHAPTER 5 · *THE REBIRTH*

IN 2011, DC COMICS DECIDED TO REBRAND its titles in a company-wide shake-up, the likes of which had not been seen since the original *Crisis on Infinite Earths* series. This initiative, called "The New 52," saw the release of fifty-two titles, each starting with a new number one issue. This meant that for the first time since 1938, *Action Comics* was restarted with issue #1. *Superman* was once again restarted, and Supergirl and Superboy also were awarded their own titles.

With this renumbering came significant changes for both Clark Kent and the *Daily Planet*. In the new *Action Comics* #1 (November 2011), a younger Clark's adventures were explored. Much like his Golden Age counterpart, this version of Clark Kent could not yet fly. He also found employment not at the upscale *Daily Planet*, but at its rather meager competitor, the *Daily Star*. While he was friends with *Daily Planet* employees Lois Lane and Jimmy Olsen, it took Clark a while before he made the transition to the staff of Metropolis's favorite newspaper.

Meanwhile, the pages of *Superman* reflected Clark Kent's modern adventures. He wore a new armored Superman suit and worked at the *Daily Planet* (once again owned by Morgan Edge), and yet this version of Clark had never been married to Lois Lane. In the first issue of Superman's third ongoing series, the comic began with a brief history of the *Daily Planet*. The *Daily Planet* building was revealed to have been constructed in 1826 as little more than a humble three-story converted warehouse. This issue then saw the introduction of a new *Daily Planet* building, as the original was razed during a public ceremony meant to celebrate Edge's purchase of the paper. In later issues, Clark would take a hiatus from working at the *Daily Planet* and start an internet news site with Cat Grant called Clarkcatropolis.com.

For all the turmoil in his career, Clark's life as Superman was even rockier in "The New 52." He battled Doomsday and defeated the villain, began a romance with Wonder Woman, and soon suffered from a severe dose of Kryptonite poisoning. His condition was so dire that, in an unexpected twist, Superman died in the pages of *Superman* #52 (July 2016). While the nation mourned the loss of Superman, another Man of Steel lurked in the shadows.

After fifty-two issues of "The New 52" initiative, DC once again shook up its comic book landscape in 2016. This time, the event was dubbed "Rebirth." As Superman's series was once again restarted at issue #1 while *Action Comics* regained its original numbering, a strangely familiar Clark Kent stepped back into the role of the Man of Steel. The married Clark Kent from the previous version of continuity had already been revealed to be secretly living in "The New 52" after a crossover event called "Convergence." So when the "New 52" Superman died, that old familiar Clark regained his Superman mantle, albeit with a few tweaks in the costume. While he has not yet regained his job at the *Daily Planet*, Superman's marriage to Lois has never been stronger. In fact, the two now have a young son named Jonathan, who stepped into the role of Superboy. He's currently showcased in the pages of his team-up title *Super Sons*, with Batman's son, Robin. And while Superman continues the fight for truth and justice, Clark Kent is clearly champing at the bit to get back to his life's other passion. It's only a matter of time before the hero returns to the field of journalism.

CONCLUSION

THROUGHOUT HISTORY, NEWSPAPERS have served as a source of truth in the world. They inform the public of events both tragic and celebratory, uncover corruption in business and politics, and help determine the topics of conversation in every office across the country. It is this industry that inspired Jerry Siegel and Joe Shuster to drop Clark Kent immediately into the chaotic life of a newspaperman. This gave Superman not just access to breaking news as it happened, but also a voice in a tumultuous world. Clark Kent became Superman's own narrator, and his paper, the *Daily Planet*, became his soapbox.

To an orphan from outer space, a country boy given a new start in the city, and a hero looking for supporters and likeminded individuals to help him fight his dangerous mission, the *Daily Planet* became a port in the storm. The paper's iconic building towers over Metropolis, a tourist attraction in the fictional town that impresses locals and visitors alike. For a citizen of the DC Universe, perhaps the only greater thrill than spying the iconic planet logo atop the Metropolis skyline is catching a glimpse of its protector flying overhead.

NOT A BIRD. NOT A PLANE. BUT SUPERMAN.

MAKE IT YOUR OWN

Feel free to unleash your creative genius as you customize your model. Start by making a plan. Anything goes! You can also follow the craft ideas here to make something totally incredible!

REPLICA

The Daily Planet has seen many incarnations since introduced to comic readers over seventy-five years ago. Still, the classic gold globe is always a good look. For this model, paint it assembled but without the letters attached yet. You can add those once it's dry.

WHAT YOU NEED:
› Paints (silver, beige, light gold, and dark gold)
› Paintbrush

Using a fine paintbrush, paint in the continents with dark gold and the oceans with light gold. Finish off the building with beige walls and silver windows. For the letters, pick one shade of gold and paint those. Attach when dry.

RUSTED/DAMAGED GLOBE

As a popular landmark of the DC Universe, the Daily Planet has taken its fair share of beatings. These moments are powerful and memorable for Superman readers, so go ahead and pay tribute to these notable times by creating a replica of a damaged, but still dignified, Daily Planet globe.

WHAT YOU NEED:

› Paints (gold, gray, white, black, silver, brown, yellow, and orange)
› Glue
› Paintbrush

WHAT YOU MIGHT WANT:

› Black chalk and stump or cotton swab
› White cardstock

Paint the globe gold, and then paint the building gray. Remove a few plates from the globe and paint the interior parts black. Paint the exposed edges silver. Using a watered-down dark brown paint, fill in the engravings on the globe. Then add the x markings on each plate. Paint more damage with un-thinned dark brown paint. Paint the fronts of the letters white. Then, make them crooked and glue into place.

For the building, use dark gray and black to add details. Paint the flames in white and then yellow and orange. For flames that go over the building, use a cut-out piece of cardstock and glue into place. For more dirt and grime, apply black chalk with a stump or cotton swab until you get the look you desire.

SUPERMAN COLORS

Everyone knows that Superman is the lifeblood of the Daily Planet—whether he's making headlines through his heroic adventures or reporting the news of the day as Clark Kent. What better way to show the Man of Steel's influence over the Daily Planet than to cover it in his bright red, blue, and yellow logo?

Print out a small version of the Superman emblem to use as a stencil. Rub a no. 2 pencil all over the back of the paper. Then cut the emblem out and tape it to the globe. Trace the image with your pencil to create a guide for you to paint. Continue by painting the emblem and then painting the globe blue, the letters white, and the equator axis gold. Finish by painting the building a light brown.

WHAT YOU NEED:

› Paints (red, yellow, blue, white, gold, and brown)
› Printout of Superman emblem
› No. 2 pencil

IncrediBuilds™
A Division of Insight Editions, LP
PO Box 3088
San Rafael, CA 94912
www.insighteditions.com
www.incredibuilds.com

  Find us on Facebook: www.facebook.com/InsightEditions
 Follow us on Twitter: @insighteditions

Library of Congress Cataloging-in-Publication Data available.

ISBN: 978-1-68298-107-8

Publisher: Raoul Goff
Associate Publisher: Jon Goodspeed
Art Director: Chrissy Kwasnik
Designer: Alison Corn
Senior Editor: Katie Kubert
Managing Editor: Alan Kaplan
Editorial Assistant: Hilary VandenBroek
Production Editor: Carly Chillmon
Associate Production Manager: Sam Taylor
Product Development Manager: Rebekah Piatte
Model Designer: Wu Zihang, TeamGreen

Insight Editions, in association with Roots of Peace, will plant two
trees for each tree used in the manufacturing of this book. Roots
of Peace is an internationally renowned humanitarian organization
dedicated to eradicating land mines worldwide and converting
war-torn lands into productive farms and wildlife habitats. Roots
of Peace will plant two million fruit and nut trees in Afghanistan
and provide farmers there with the skills and support necessary for
sustainable land use.

MANUFACTURED IN CHINA

10 9 8 7 6 5 4 3 2 1

SOURCES

1: Daniels, Les. *DC Comics: Sixty Years of the
World's Favorite Comic Book Heroes.* Boston:
Little Brown, 1995.

2: Ludlam, George Putnam. "The Baby from
Krypton." *The Adventures of Superman.* New
York City: WOR. February 12, 1940.

ABOUT THE AUTHOR

Matthew K. Manning is the writer of the
best-selling crossover *Batman/Teenage
Mutant Ninja Turtles Adventures*, recently
nominated for Comic of the Year by the
Diamond Gem Awards. During the course
of his career, Manning has served as a
regular writer for the titles *TMNT: New
Animated Adventures*, *TMNT Amazing
Adventures*, *Beware the Batman*, *The Batman
Strikes!*, and *Legion of Super-Heroes in
the 31st Century*. He has also written for
the comic book titles *Batman*, *Sensation
Comics Featuring Wonder Woman*, *Batman
80-Page Giant 2010*, *Spider-Man Unlimited*,
Justice League Adventures, *Looney Tunes*,
Scooby-Doo, and *Marvel Romance Redux*. In
addition, Manning has authored more than
fifty books starring comic book characters
or examining the rich history of comic
books themselves. Some of his most recent
books include the Amazon best seller from
DK Publishing *Batman: A Visual History* and
Andrews McMeel's acclaimed coffee table
books, *The Batman Files* and *The Superman
Files*. Visit him online at
www.matthewkmanning.com.

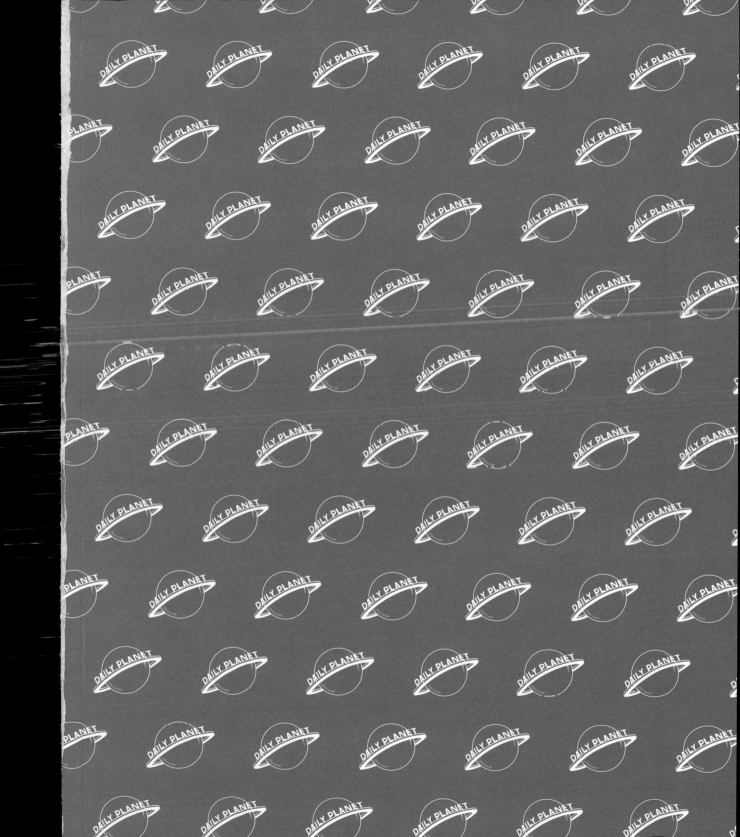

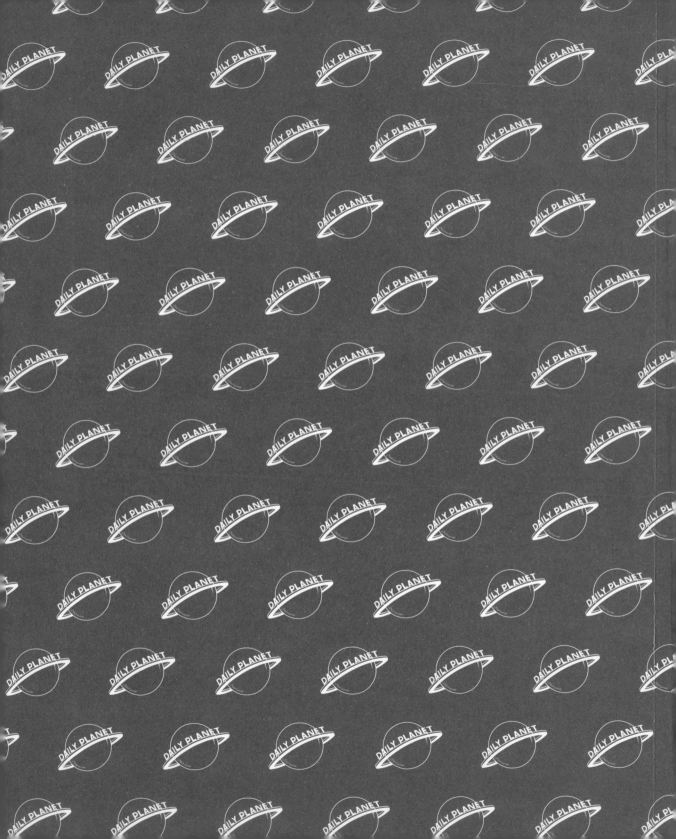